STAR WARS® ADVENTURES

BOBA FETT AND THE SHIP OF FEAR

Designer
Aimee Danielson-Germany

Assistant Editor
Freddye Lins

Editor
Randy Stradley

President and Publisher
Mike Richardson

Special thanks to Jann Moorhead, David Anderman, Troy Alders, Leland Chee, Sue Rostoni, and Carol Roeder at Lucas Licensing

STAR WARS ADVENTURES: BOBA FETT AND THE SHIP OF FEAR

Published by
Dark Horse Books
A division of Dark Horse Comics, Inc.
10956 SE Main Street
Milwaukie, OR 97222

darkhorse.com
starwars.com

To find a comics shop in your area, call the Comic Shop Locator Service toll-free at 1-888-266-4226

Barlow, Jeremy.
Boba Fett and the ship of fear / script, Jeremy Barlow ; art, Daxiong ; lettering, Michael Heisler ; cover art Sean McNally. -- 1st ed.
p. cm. -- (Star Wars adventures)
ISBN 978-1-59582-436-3
1. Graphic novels. I. Daxiong, 1975- II. McNally, Sean. III. Title.
PZ7.7.B36Bo 2011
741.5'973--dc22

2010034011

First edition: May 2011
ISBN 978-1-59582-436-3

10 9 8 7 6 5 4 3 2 1
Printed by Midas Printing International, Ltd., Huizhou, China.

BOBA FETT AND THE SHIP OF FEAR

Script **Jeremy Barlow**

Art **Daxiong**

Lettering **Michael Heisler**

Cover **Sean McNally**

Dark Horse Books®

THIS STORY TAKES PLACE APPROXIMATELY TWO YEARS AFTER THE BATTLE OF YAVIN.

AN AMBUSH...?
WHO...?

OLD HALLET PRAIRIE.
DOLVA PRIME, IN THE MID RIM.
I'D LEAVE THAT BLASTER IN ITS HOLSTER, IF I WERE YOU.
YOU...
OF COURSE.

YOU'RE NOT ME.
YOU'RE RIGHT ABOUT THAT.
CHAK!
TOK!

SO THIS IS HOW IT IS? WE DO THE HARD WORK OF STEALING THAT THING, AND YOU JUST COME ALONG AND TAKE IT FROM US?
SOMETHING LIKE THAT.

IT'S NOT YOURS TO TAKE, *FETT.*
YOU'RE STEALING OUR LIVELIHOODS HERE. *EDO* AND I EARNED THIS ONE -- WE *NEED* IT.

BECAUSE UNLIKE YOU, I DON'T WORRY ABOUT WHO I **AM** OR WHAT I'M ***SUPPOSED*** TO BE. I JUST GET THE JOB DONE --

-- AND I WANTED THIS ONE ***MORE*** THAN YOU DID.

NOW GO PULL YOUR BROTHER OUT OF THIS WRECK AND CHAIN YOURSELVES TO IT.

YOU THINK YOU ***KNOW*** US. YOU DON'T KNOW ***ANYTHING.***

MAYBE NOT.
BUT I DO KNOW THAT I'M NOT SO DESPERATE...

...THAT I CAN'T TELL THIS ARACHEDRON SCULPTURE IS A FAKE.

KROOM!

THAT DOESN'T MEAN IT'S *WORTHLESS...*

...IT'S WHAT'S *INSIDE* THAT INTERESTS ME.

WE'RE DONE HERE.
I'LL BE SEEING YOU STROM BROTHERS AROUND.

YOU'RE LEAVING US HERE TO *BURN?*
ROLU? WHAT'S HAPPENING?

WHOEVER YOU TOOK THAT SCULPTURE FROM IS PROBABLY AFTER YOU.
MAYBE THEY'LL CATCH UP TO YOU BEFORE THE FIRE DOES.

YOU'RE KILLING US HERE! WHY NOT JUST SHOOT US WHILE YOU'RE AT IT?

BECAUSE THERE'S NO MONEY IN IT.

YOU'LL WISH YOU HAD. SOONER OR LATER, LEAVING US ALIVE IS GOING TO COST YOU.
IT'S GOING TO COST YOU *BIG*.

I'LL TAKE MY CHANCES.

DENOV, DO YOU READ ME?
LOUD AND CLEAR, BOSS.
I NEED YOU TO FIND THE LAST KNOWN WHEREABOUTS OF A SHIP CALLED THE *REVERIE.*

NEVER HEARD OF IT. WHAT DO YOU WANT WITH --
REVERIE...

JUST DO IT.
WE'RE NOT FINISHED HERE, FETT...

"...NOT BY A LONG SHOT."

SHORTLY...

WHAT DO YOU HAVE FOR ME?

I FOUND IT -- BUT I FOUND **SOMETHING ELSE** EVEN BETTER...

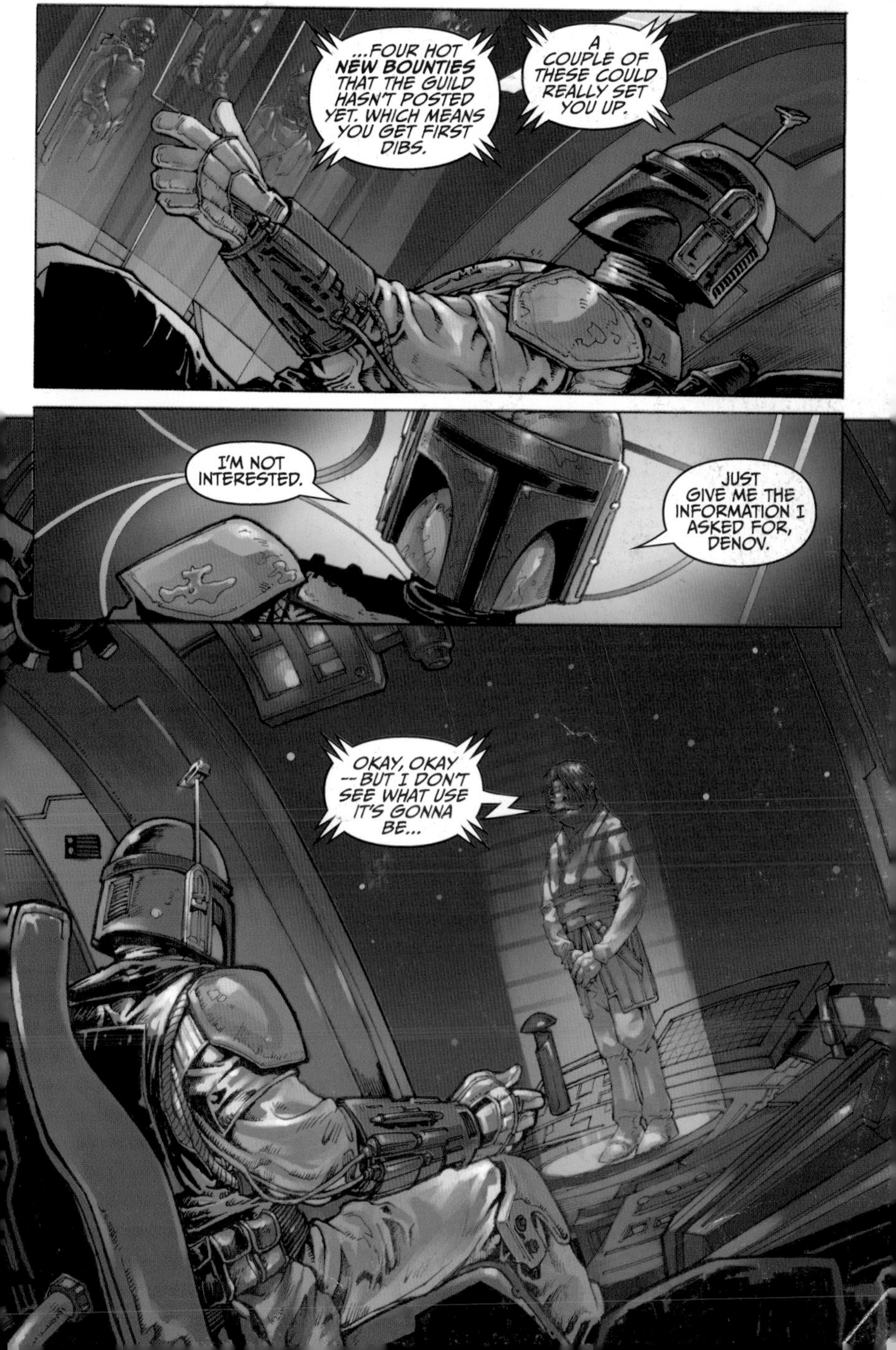

...FOUR HOT **NEW BOUNTIES** THAT THE GUILD HASN'T POSTED YET. WHICH MEANS YOU GET FIRST DIBS.
A COUPLE OF THESE COULD REALLY SET YOU UP.

I'M NOT INTERESTED.

JUST GIVE ME THE INFORMATION I ASKED FOR, DENOV.

OKAY, OKAY --BUT I DON'T SEE WHAT USE IT'S GONNA BE...

"IN ITS DAY -- WE'RE TALKING FOUR HUNDRED YEARS AGO -- THE REVERIE WAS A TOP-OF-THE-LINE LUXURY CRUISER.
"RUMOR HAS IT SIX PLANETS WENT BROKE SPENDING TO BUILD IT.
"I DON'T KNOW ABOUT THAT -- BUT I DO KNOW THAT IT CATERED TO THE RICHEST PEOPLE IN THE GALAXY.
"JUST BUYING A TICKET COST MORE MONEY THAN WE'LL EVER SEE...
"...OR I'LL EVER SEE, ANYWAY.

"THING IS, FOR AS MUCH AS THEY SPENT ON MAKING HER LOOK PRETTY, THEY CUT CORNERS ON THE LITTLE THINGS --
"-- SMALL DETAILS LIKE FIRE CONTROLS AND SHIELDING SYSTEMS.
"A COUPLE YEARS INTO HER VOYAGE, SOMETHING BREACHED HER HULL AND -- WHOOP! -- DOWN SHE WENT."
I DIDN'T ASK FOR A HISTORY LESSON -- JUST TELL ME WHERE IT IS.

"AFTER THE ACCIDENT, SHE CHANGED HANDS A FEW TIMES. NO ONE COULD AFFORD THE UPKEEP, LET ALONE THE OVERHAUL SHE NEEDED TO FLY AGAIN...
"...SO THE OWNERS DID THE *RESPONSIBLE* AND *HONORABLE* THING...
"...THEY STRIPPED HER VALUABLES AND DUMPED HER AT A MASSIVE *SHIP GRAVEYARD* WAY OUT ON THE GALAXY'S EDGE.
"OUT OF SIGHT, OUT OF MIND, RIGHT?

"FOLKS HAVE BEEN DITCHING THEIR TRASH OUT THERE FOR CENTURIES, SO GOOD LUCK SPOTTING *THE REVERIE* IN THAT MESS...

"...IF YOU ***DO*** GET LUCKY AND FIND HER ON ONE OF THE JUNK FIELD'S OUTER EDGES, CHANCES ARE YOU WON'T BE ALONE...

"...YOU'LL HAVE TO DEAL WITH THE *JUNKERS* AND SCRAP MERCHANTS. THIEVES, THE LOT OF 'EM.
KUNK!
GRIND! GRIND! GRIND!
"THESE GUYS CHEW THEIR WAY THROUGH SHIPYARDS LIKE THIS, BLASTING AWAY HULL CHUNKS AND DRAGGING THE PIECES INTO THEIR SHIP GRINDERS.
"IF THESE GUYS ARE WORKING ON *THE REVERIE*, WHATEVER YOU GOTTA DO, YOU BETTER DO IT QUICK--
"--BECAUSE SHE WON'T BE IN ONE PIECE FOR LONG."

AND THAT WOULD BE...

NOT YOUR CONCERN.

DO YOU HAVE THE SHIP'S SCHEMATICS?

HR-CHAK
HR-CHAK

SORT OF. JUST THE CONCEPT DESIGNS THEY PITCHED TO THE INVESTORS.
THEY MIGHT BE MORE WISHFUL THINKING THAN ACTUAL WORK PRINTS.

THAT'LL HAVE TO DO. I NEED YOU TO GUIDE ME TOWARD THE SHIP'S SECURITY VAULTS.

NOT SURE IF THE POWER GENERATORS STILL WORK AFTER ALL THIS TIME, BUT IT'S WORTH A TRY.
PROBABLY BE A LOT EASIER FOR YOU TO MOVE AROUND WITH THE LIGHTS ON.

UH, ASSUMING THESE DIAGRAMS ARE KSSH! **CLOSE** TO ACCURATE, YOU KSSH! BE COMING UP ON THE **ENGINEERING DECKS.**
LOOK FOR A CONTROL CONSOLE WITH KSSSHH! OR A LEVER OF SOME KIND. THAT SHOULD FIRE UP THE GENERATORS.

FIND IT?
FOUND **SOMETHING.** BUT I'M LOSING **YOU** -- YOUR SIGNAL'S BREAKING UP. I'M CUTTING THE COMM.
KSSSH! YOU SURE ABOUT THAT?

CHA-CHUNK!

I HATE TO
≡KSSH!≡ THINK OF
YOU ALL ALONE
OUT THERE.
SKITTER 
SKITTER
SKITTER
SKITTER

SQUEE!
SQUEE!
SQUEE!
SQUEE!

KER-CHAW!
SPLOOCH!

SSAAAA!

FWOOSH!
SKEEE!

K'DEW!
K'DEW!

OVER HERE-- HURRY!
THIS ROOM IS SEALED! WE CAN KEEP THEM OUT!

KDEW!
KDEW!

KDEW!
KDEW!
KDEW!

HIT
HIM!

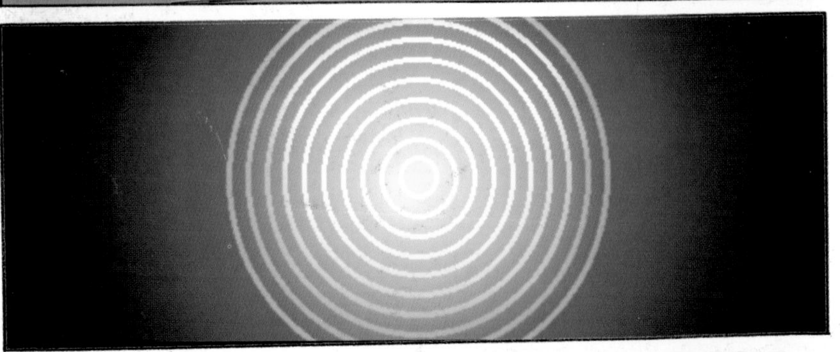

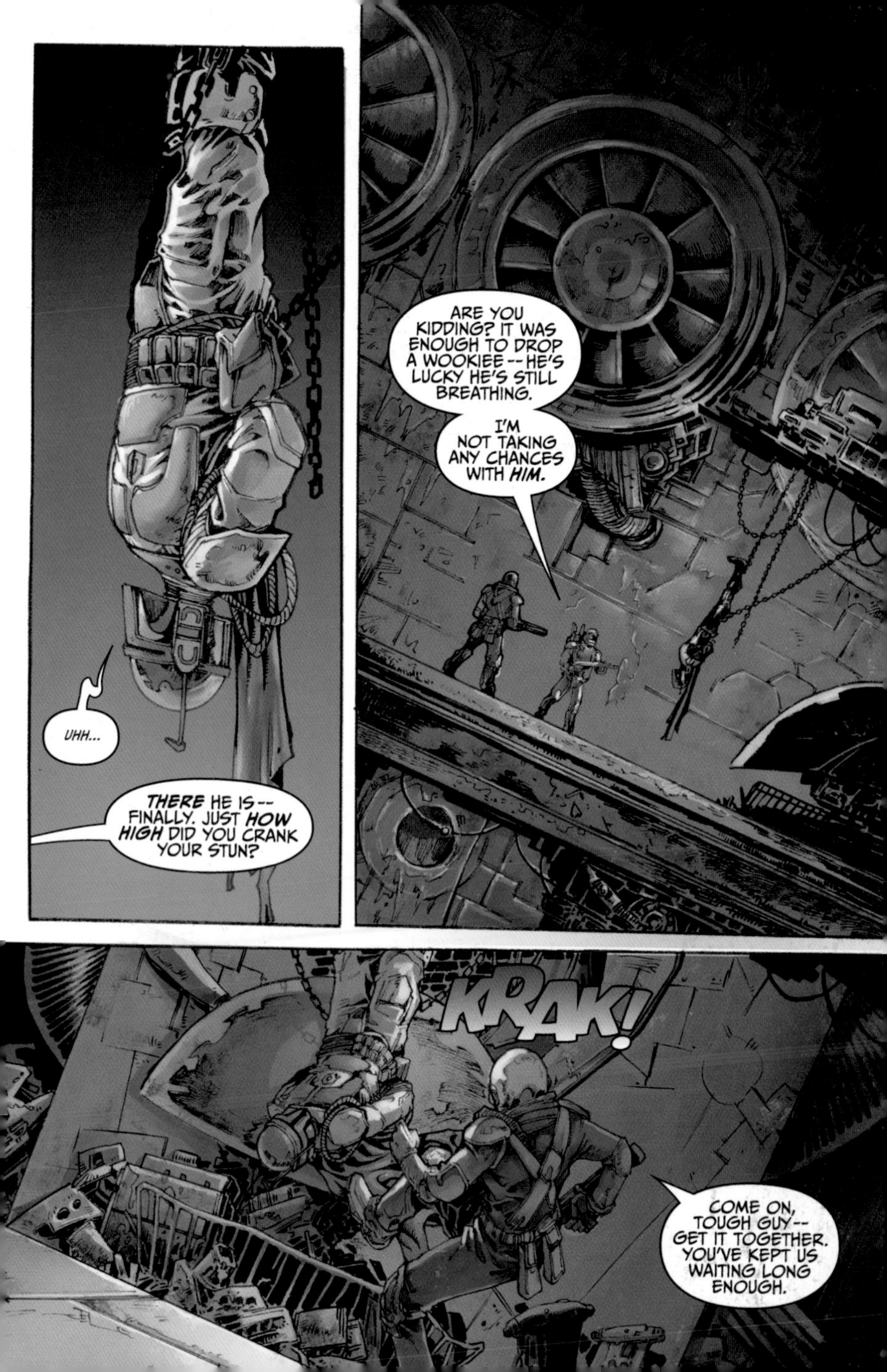

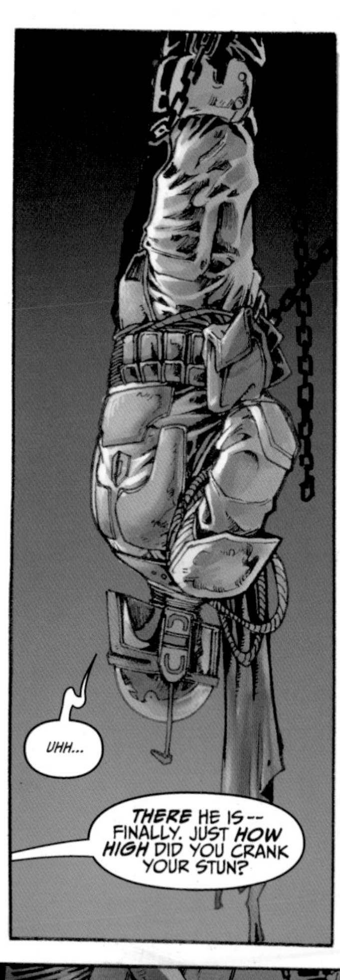
UHH...
THERE HE IS-- FINALLY. JUST HOW HIGH DID YOU CRANK YOUR STUN?

ARE YOU KIDDING? IT WAS ENOUGH TO DROP A WOOKIEE--HE'S LUCKY HE'S STILL BREATHING.
I'M NOT TAKING ANY CHANCES WITH HIM.

KRAK!
COME ON, TOUGH GUY-- GET IT TOGETHER. YOU'VE KEPT US WAITING LONG ENOUGH.

YOU MUST BE IN A HURRY TO DIE, THEN.
YOU CRACK ME UP, FETT...

...YOU *HAD* YOUR CHANCE TO KILL US...
TCHAK!

...AND YOU *BLEW* IT.

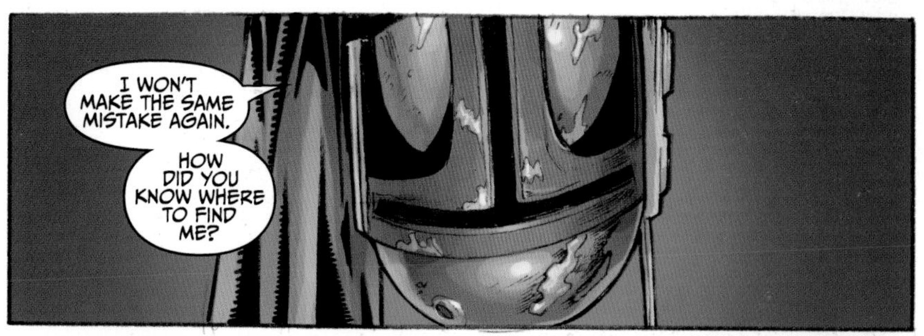
I WON'T MAKE THE SAME MISTAKE AGAIN.
HOW DID YOU KNOW WHERE TO FIND ME?

LET'S JUST SAY YOU'RE NOT THE ONLY ONE WITH A MOLE INSIDE THE BOUNTY HUNTERS' GUILD.
DON'T LISTEN TO 'IM, BOSS -- I HAD NOTHING TO DO WITH THIS!

IT WAS FAIRLY OBVIOUS, THOUGH -- ONCE WE HEARD YOU SAY THE NAME OF THIS SHIP, WE PUT TWO AND TWO TOGETHER.
YOU WERE RIGHT. OUR ARACHEDRON WAS A PHONY...

"...AND *YOU'RE* AFTER THE *REAL* DEAL.

"ACCORDING TO LEGEND, THE ARACHEDRON WAS CENTRAL TO SOME ALIEN CULTURE THAT'S LONG SINCE DIED OUT.

"BUT AS THESE THINGS DO, THE SACRED RELICS BECAME VALUABLE TRINKETS FOR THE WEALTHY.
"IT'D PROBABLY STILL BE GATHERING DUST IN SOME MANSION RIGHT NOW...

"...IF IT WEREN'T CURSED."

IF YOU *BELIEVE* IN THAT JUNK, I MEAN. CAN'T SAY I DO, BUT YOU HAVE TO WONDER...
...IF IT HADN'T BEEN ABOARD *THE REVERIE* ON HER FINAL FLIGHT -- WOULD THE ACCIDENT HAVE HAPPENED?

IF THE ARACHEDRON EXISTS, IT'LL BE WORTH *MILLIONS.*
FOR ABOUT A HUNDRED YEARS OR SO AFTER THE ACCIDENT, FORTUNE HUNTERS FROM HERE TO *NAR SHADDAA* SET OUT TO PILLAGE HER HALLS...

...NONE CAME BACK ALIVE. WHICH MEANS YOU'RE NOT THE FIRST ONE WHO'S GOING TO DIE HERE, FETT.
BUT YOU *WILL* BE THE LAST.

THIS IS A BIG MOMENT FOR YOU AND YOUR BROTHER, EDO.

MAYBE YOU'LL FINALLY EARN THE ***RESPECT*** YOU'VE BEEN CHASING SO LONG.

MAYBE YOU WON'T LIVE SO DEEP IN YOUR FATHER'S SHADOW ANYMORE. THAT HAS TO FEEL GOOD.
YOUR DAD WAS ONE OF THE BEST THERE WAS -- I RESPECTED HIM. BECAUSE OF THAT, I WON'T SPOIL THIS FOR YOU. NOT YET, ANYWAY.
SO TAKE IT IN. ENJOY THIS MOMENT FOR ALL OF THE POTENTIAL IT PROMISES -- BECAUSE IT'S ALMOST PAST.

YOU'RE ABOUT TO REALIZE A HARD AND UNAVOIDABLE TRUTH...

...THERE'S **NO WAY** YOU'RE GETTING OFF THIS SHIP WITHOUT MY HELP.

KSSSS!

KSSSS!
?
JUST SHOOT 'EM!
BDOW!
BDOW!
BDOW!
BDOW!

KKSSSAAAHH!!

SPLORCH!

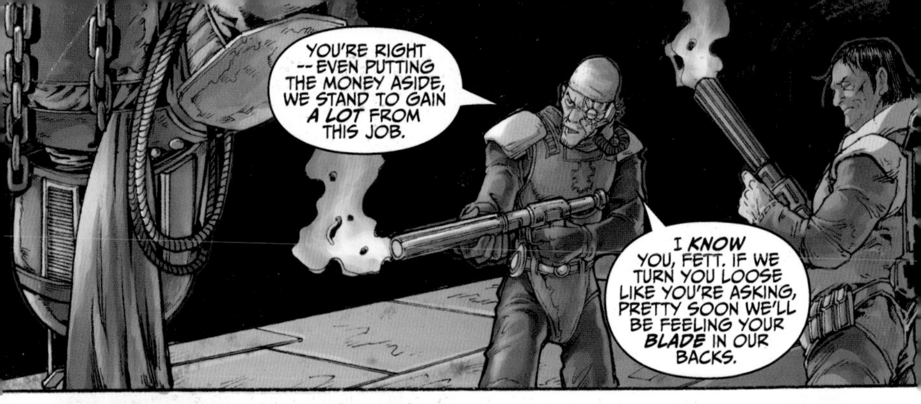
YOU'RE RIGHT --EVEN PUTTING THE MONEY ASIDE, WE STAND TO GAIN *A LOT* FROM THIS JOB.
I *KNOW* YOU, FETT. IF WE TURN YOU LOOSE LIKE YOU'RE ASKING, PRETTY SOON WE'LL BE FEELING YOUR *BLADE* IN OUR BACKS.

GIVE ME *ONE GOOD REASON* WHY I CAN TRUST THAT *WON'T* HAPPEN.

THERE ISN'T ONE. BUT I CAN'T GET THROUGH THIS SHIP'S INFESTATION ON MY OWN, EITHER --I NEED YOU AS MUCH AS YOU NEED ME.

GOOD ENOUGH FOR ME.
EDO-- UNLOCK HIM.

WE TOOK YOUR JETPACK'S FUEL CELLS AND THREW YOUR RIFLE OVER THE SIDE.
TAKE THESE -- THEY'LL WORK IN A PINCH. THEY'RE KEYED TO OUR BIO-SIGNATURES, SO YOU CAN USE THEM, BUT YOU CAN'T USE THEM AGAINST *US*.

LET'S GET MOVING.

CLICK! CLICK!

HEY!
I HAD TO KNOW I COULD TRUST WHAT YOU SAY.

KRA-KROOOM!
RRRRUUMMBBLE!
WHAT--?!
IT'S THE JUNKERS-- THEY'RE ALMOST ON US. WON'T BE LONG BEFORE THIS WHOLE SHIP COMES APART.

RRRRUMMBBLLE!

RRUMMMBBLE!

MAKE FOR THAT REPULSOR-LIFT!

NNGGHH!!
KDEW!

TIME TO GO!
KDEW!
KDEW!

KDEW!
KDEW!

WE SHOULD KEEP MOVING --BEFORE THOSE THINGS FIND A WAY IN HERE.
WHERE'S THE LIFT'S CAB?

WE'RE STANDING ON IT.

NOWHERE TO GO BUT UP.

TELL ME SOMETHING, FETT...
...YOU SAY YOU RESPECTED OUR FATHER.
YOU KNOW HE THOUGHT *YOU* WERE SCUM, RIGHT?

I ADMIRED *PHILO STROM*. DOESN'T MEAN I ALWAYS AGREED WITH HIM.

THAT'S OBVIOUS.
YOU NEVER WERE ONE TO BOTHER WITH LITTLE THINGS LIKE INTEGRITY OR *HONOR*.

YOU STROMS...YOU NEVER *COULD* TELL THE DIFFERENCE BETWEEN HONOR AND *COMMON SENSE.*

COMMON SENSE? *THAT'S* HOW YOU JUSTIFY ALL YOUR LYING AND DOUBLE-DEALING?

WE'RE FAR FROM SAINTS, BUT WE KNOW WHERE THE LINE IS AND WE DON'T CROSS IT.

RIGHT. YOU WERE ABOUT TO LEAVE ME TO *DIE* IN THE ENGINE ROOM BACK THERE.
IF THE ROLES WERE REVERSED, YOU'D HAVE DONE THE SAME TO US.

HEY, YOU *DID* DO THE SAME THING TO US!

CALL IT WHAT YOU WANT-- JUST STOP BLAMING ME FOR YOUR SHORTCOMINGS.
YOUR OLD MAN WAS GOOD, NO DOUBT ABOUT IT...
...HE DID WHAT IT TOOK TO GET THE JOB DONE, AND SOMEHOW KEPT HIS HANDS CLEAN IN THE PROCESS.
BUT YOU TWO...
...YOU'RE DECENT BOUNTY HUNTERS -- YOU MIGHT EVEN BE GREAT SOMEDAY -- BUT NOT WHILE THE WEIGHT OF YOUR LEGACY DRAGS YOU DOWN.
AND IT'S YOUR OWN FAULT-- YOU EXPLOITED YOUR FAMILY NAME -- YOU PLAYED UP EXPECTATIONS THAT NO ONE COULD MEET.
NOW EVERY JOB YOU TAKE IS A FIGHT FOR LEGITIMACY AND RESPECT THAT YOU CAN'T SEEM TO WIN. I'D BE BITTER ABOUT IT, TOO.

IF YOU THINK KILLING ME AND WALKING OUT OF HERE WITH THE ARACHEDRON WILL CHANGE THAT, YOU'RE WRONG.

I'LL TAKE MY CHANCES.

OKAY, THAT SETTLES IT...
...I'M OFFICIALLY CREEPED OUT.

GAH! MORE BUGS!
WAIT...
HEY--!

...THEY'RE NOT AFTER *US.*

WHAT ARE THEY LOOKING AT? IT'S LIKE SOMETHING HAS THEM IN A TRANCE.

"YOU AREN'T GOING TO BELIEVE THIS!

"THE GOOD NEWS IS, BY SHEER DUMB LUCK WE'VE FOUND WHAT WE CAME HERE FOR...

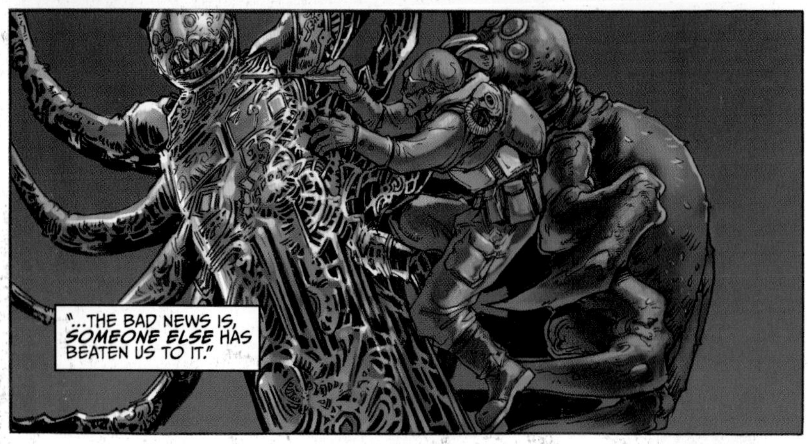
"...THE BAD NEWS IS, SOMEONE ELSE HAS BEATEN US TO IT."

I DON'T THINK SO. I'M NOT HAVING THIS THING STOLEN OUT FROM UNDER ME ***AGAIN.***

HEY, BUDDY--

-- THAT'S A REAL NICE SPIDER DISGUISE YOU'RE WEARING...
...BUT HOW 'BOUT YOU JUMP ON DOWN HERE AND HAND THAT OVER?

ARE YOU KIDDING ME?
I'VE BEEN ON THIS SHIP FOR TWO WEEKS LOOKING FOR THIS THING -- YOU CAN'T JUST COME ALONG AND SNATCH IT AWAY FROM ME.

BELIEVE ME, I KNOW HOW YOU FEEL.
BUT THAT'S EXACTLY WHAT WE'RE DOING.

RRRRRUMMMBLE!
BOOM!
I'D REALLY LIKE TO LEAVE NOW, IF THAT WORKS FOR EVERYONE.

WHY COULDN'T I HAVE GOTTEN HERE YESTERDAY?

AAAIIIIEEESSHHHKK!

KROOM!
KA-KROOM!
BRA-KRAKA-KOOM!

RRRUUMMBBLE!
KROOM!
KDEW!
THERE'S TOO MANY OF THEM!
KDEW!
KDEW!
RRRUMMBBLLE!

IT'S NOT *US* THEY WANT. IT'S THIS ARTIFACT -- IT HAS SOME WEIRD HOLD OVER THEM.
WELL, THEY AREN'T GETTING IT. I HAVE *MORE* THAN ENOUGH AMMO TO GO AROUND.

THE ONLY WAY OUT IS THE WAY WE CAME IN -- WE HAVE TO CLEAR A PATH!
KDEW!
KDEW!
KDEW!

THAT'S NOT HAPPENING -- NOT UNLESS YOU WANT TO SWIM THROUGH THAT SEA OF SPIDERS TO GET THERE.
WE HAVE TO FIND ANOTHER WAY OUT, AND WE HAVE TO DO IT QUICK!

KDEW!
KDEW!
KDEW!
I DON'T WANT TO DIE HERE, ROLU!

NEITHER DO I.

THAT OLD RELIC ISN'T WORTH ALL OF THIS.
GIVE IT TO ME.

HNNGRAAGH!!

WHAT DID YOU JUST DO?!

BRA-KOOM!!
FWA-WHOOOSH

SOK!
I JUST SAVED OUR LIVES.

I'M NO TREASURE HUNTER. I DON'T CARE *WHAT* THIS THING WAS--ONLY WHAT IT'S *WORTH...*

...AND IT WASN'T WORTH MORE THAN *STAYING ALIVE.*

THIS WAS JUST ANOTHER JOB FOR YOU, BUT FOR *US*...
YOU HAVEN'T *SAVED* OUR LIVES -- YOU'VE *DESTROYED* THEM.

USE YOUR HEAD --

-- YOU THINK I'VE MADE IT THIS FAR BY TAKING STUPID CHANCES?

FORGET YOU!
I'M NOT GIVING UP ON THIS. I WON'T LEAVE HERE WITHOUT THE ARACHEDRON...

...AND NEITHER WOULD OUR FATHER.

ROLU-- WHAT ARE YOU *DOING?!*
NO!!

KDEW! KDEW! KDEW!

HERE -- YOUR JETPACK'S FUEL CELLS ARE INSIDE.
YOU WERE RIGHT ALL ALONG.

DON'T BE CRAZY! YOU'RE NOT GOING AFTER HIM!

I HAVE TO. HE'S MY BROTHER...
...HE'S ALL I HAVE LEFT.

KKRR
UUMMMBBLE!

I'VE HAD MORE THAN ENOUGH OF THIS PLACE. GOOD LUCK GETTING BACK TO YOUR SHIP.
I'LL PAY YOU *FIFTY THOUSAND* CREDITS TO GET ME OUT OF HERE!

CHA-CHIK!

I WAS THINKING A *HUNDRED* SOUNDED BETTER.
FINE! FINE -- OKAY!

BRAKA-
BRAKA-
KROOOM!
THEN WE HAVE A DEAL.
KKRRRUUMMBBLE!
KROOM-
KROOM!

STRAP YOURSELF IN -- THIS MIGHT GET ROUGH.

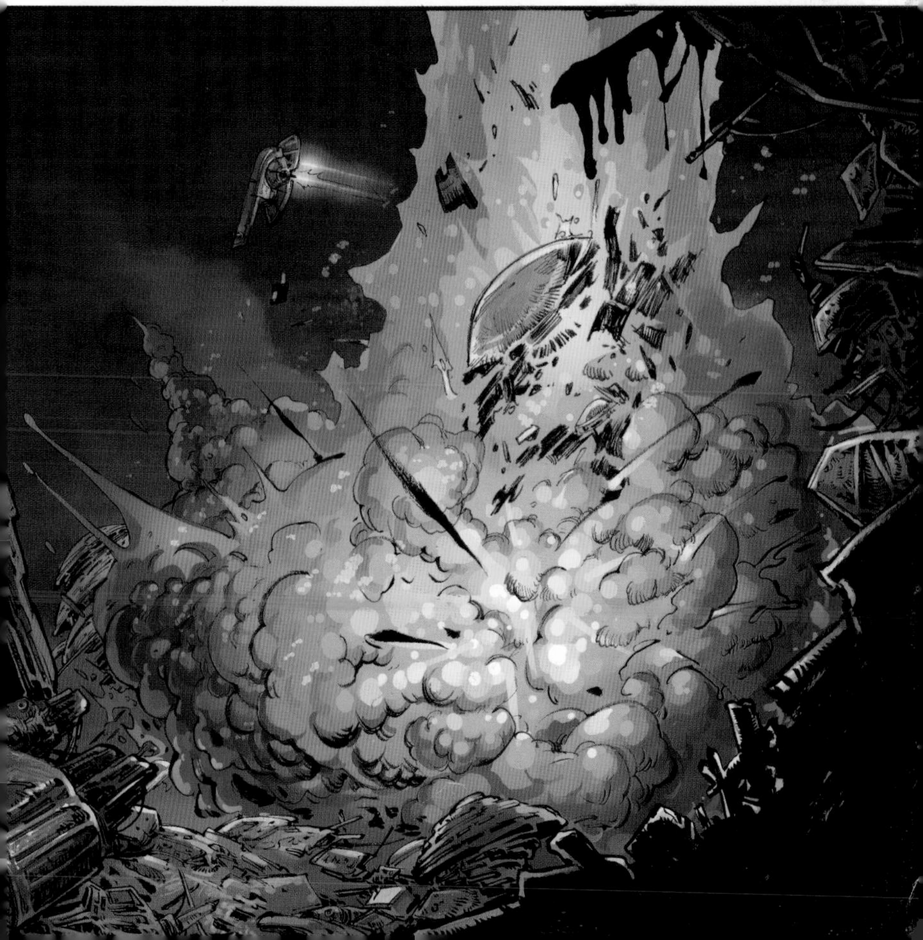

EVENTUALLY...
...THERE. THE FUNDS HAVE BEEN TRANSFERRED TO YOUR ACCOUNT -- ONE HUNDRED THOUSAND CREDITS. THAT ABOUT CLEANS ME OUT.
BUT I'D RATHER BE BROKE AND ALIVE THAN THE ALTERNATIVE.

IT SCARES ME A LITTLE, WHAT THOSE BROTHERS DID -- THROWING THEIR LIVES AWAY LIKE THAT.
I'VE SPENT A GOOD PART OF MY ADULT LIFE CHASING THAT ARACHEDRON. I MIGHT'VE CHASED IT INTO THE ABYSS RIGHT ALONG WITH THEM.

THAT MAKES ONE OF US. THE STROMS NEVER UNDERSTOOD THAT A BOUNTY HUNTER'S GREATEST ASSET ISN'T CUNNING -- IT'S SOUND JUDGMENT.

WHEN THE REWARD IS NO LONGER WORTH THE RISK, YOU CUT IT LOOSE.
IT'S AN UNFORGIVING LESSON...AND THEY LEARNED IT THE HARD WAY.

STILL... FINDING THE ARACHEDRON WAS A ONCE-IN-A-LIFETIME.
YOU THREW AWAY A FORTUNE BACK THERE, YOU KNOW THAT?
EVEN WITH THAT ***BUNDLE*** I JUST WIRED TO YOU, YOU MUST FEEL LIKE YOU TOOK A MAJOR HIT ON THIS JOB.

NOT EXACTLY...
...I DO STILL HAVE ***YOU.***

AND THE BOUNTY ON YOU, ***SOMAZ,*** IS WORTH ***ALMOST*** A FORTUNE.

"...I NEVER SAID CUNNING WASN'T IMPORTANT, TOO."

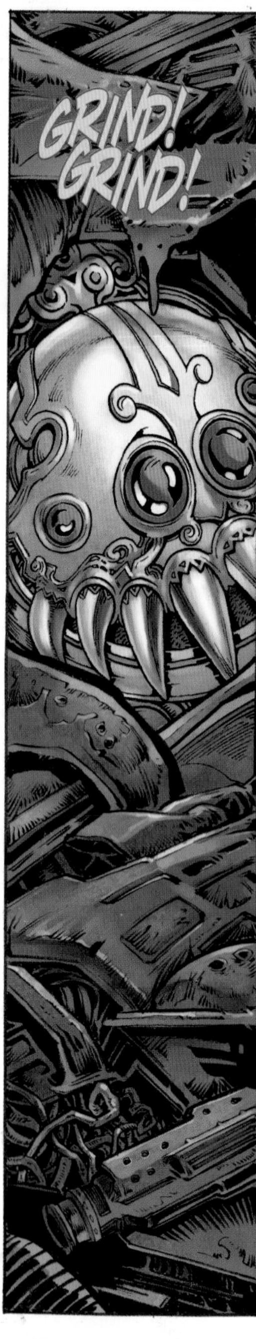
GRIND! GRIND!

GRIND!
GRIND!

KRUNCH!
THE END

STAR WARS GRAPHIC NOVEL TIMELINE (IN YEARS)

Omnibus: Tales of the Jedi—5,000–3,986 BSW4
Knights of the Old Republic—3,964–3,963 BSW4
The Old Republic—3653,3678 BSW4
Jedi vs. Sith—1,000 BSW4
Omnibus: Rise of the Sith—33 BSW4
Episode I: The Phantom Menace—32 BSW4
Omnibus: Emissaries and Assassins—32 BSW4
Twilight—31 BSW4
Bounty Hunters—31 BSW4
Omnibus: Menace Revealed—31–22 BSW4
Darkness—30 BSW4
The Stark Hyperspace War—30 BSW4
Rite of Passage—28 BSW4
Honor and Duty—24 BSW4
Episode II: Attack of the Clones—22 BSW4
Clone Wars—22–19 BSW4
Clone Wars Adventures—22–19 BSW4
General Grievous—22–19 BSW4
Episode III: Revenge of the Sith—19 BSW4
Dark Times—19 BSW4
Omnibus: Droids—5.5 BSW4
Boba Fett: Enemy of the Empire—3 BSW4
Underworld—1 BSW4
Episode IV: A New Hope—SW4
Classic Star Wars—0–3 ASW4
A Long Time Ago . . . —0–4 ASW4
Empire—0 ASW4
Rebellion—0 ASW4
Boba Fett: Man with a Mission—0 ASW4
Omnibus: Early Victories—0–3 ASW4
Jabba the Hutt: The Art of the Deal—1 ASW4
Episode V: The Empire Strikes Back—3 ASW4
Omnibus: Shadows of the Empire—3.5–4.5 ASW4
Episode VI: Return of the Jedi—4 ASW4
Omnibus: X-Wing Rogue Squadron—4–5 ASW4
Heir to the Empire—9 ASW4
Dark Force Rising—9 ASW4
The Last Command—9 ASW4
Dark Empire—10 ASW4
Boba Fett: Death, Lies, and Treachery—10 ASW4
Crimson Empire—11 ASW4
Jedi Academy: Leviathan—12 ASW4
Union—19 ASW4
Chewbacca—25 ASW4
Invasion—25 ASW4
Legacy—130–137 ASW4

Old Republic Era
25,000 – 1000 years before
Star Wars: A New Hope

Rise of the Empire Era
1000 – 0 years before
Star Wars: A New Hope

Rebellion Era
0 – 5 years after
Star Wars: A New Hope

New Republic Era
5 – 25 years after
Star Wars: A New Hope

New Jedi Order Era
25+ years after
Star Wars: A New Hope

Legacy Era
130+ years after
Star Wars: A New Hope

Infinities
Does not apply to timeline

Sergio Aragonés Stomps Star Wars
Star Wars Tales
Star Wars Infinities
Tag and Bink
Star Wars Visionaries

BSW4 = before *Episode IV: A New Hope*. ASW4 = after *Episode IV: A New Hope*.

Don't miss any of the action-packed adventures of your favorite STAR WARS® characters, available at comics shops and bookstores in a galaxy near you!

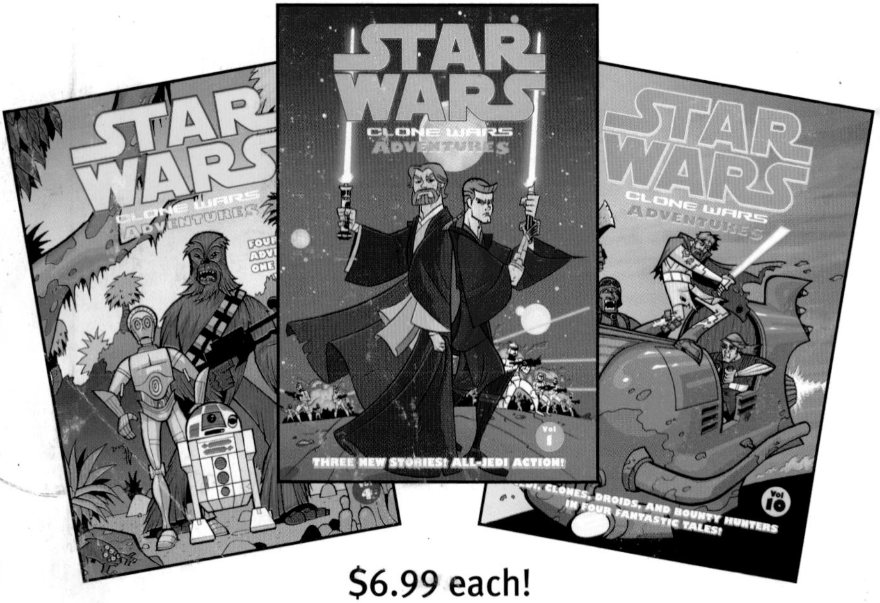

$6.99 each!

Volume 1
ISBN 978-1-59307-243-8

Volume 2
ISBN 978-1-59307-271-1

Volume 3
ISBN 978-1-59307-307-7

Volume 4
ISBN 978-1-59307-402-9

Volume 5
ISBN 978-1-59307-483-8

Volume 6
ISBN 978-1-59307-567-5

Volume 7
ISBN 978-1-59307-678-8

Volume 8
ISBN 978-1-59307-680-1

Volume 9
ISBN 978-1-59307-832-4

Volume 10
ISBN 978-1-59307-878-2

AVAILABLE AT YOUR LOCAL COMICS SHOP OR BOOKSTORE
To find a comics shop in your area, call 1-888-266-4226

For more information or to order direct: • On the web: darkhorse.com • Phone: 1-800-862-0052 Mon.–Fri. 9 AM to 5 PM Pacific Time.
• E-mail: mailorder@darkhorse.com *Prices and availability subject to change without notice.